Roaring
ROCKETS

For Danny Spiegelhalter and Virgil Tracy—T. M.

This edition produced for Baby's First Book Club®
Bristol, PA 19007.

First published in Great Britain in 1998 by Kingfisher,
an imprint of Kingfisher Publications Plc, London
2 4 6 8 10 9 7 5 3 1 (HC)

IBFBC/1101/TWP/RPR(FR)/AMA170

Text copyright © Tony Mitton 1997
Illustrations copyright © Ant Parker 1997
All rights reserved under International and Pan-American Copyright Conventions

LIBRARY OF CONGRESS CATALOGING-IN-PUBLICATION DATA
Mitton, Tony.
Roaring rockets / Tony Mitton, author; Ant Parker, illustrator
p.   cm.
Summary: A simple explanation of how space rockets work, where they travel, and what they do.
1. Rockets (Aeronautics)—Juvenile literature. [1. Rockets (Aeronautics) 2. Outer space—Exploration.]
I. Parker, Ant, ill.
II. Title.
TL782.5.M53 1997
629.47'5—dc21   97-5423 CIP AC

ISBN 1 5804 8208 2

Printed in Singapore

Roaring
ROCKETS

Tony Mitton
and
Ant Parker

Rockets have power. They rise and roar.

This rocket's waiting, ready to soar.

Rockets carry astronauts with cool white suits.

oxygen helmets, and gravity boots.

The countdown is finishing: 3, 2, 1 . . .

Action! Blast off! The journey's begun.

Rockets have fuel in great big tanks.

When they are empty, they drop away . . . thanks!

Up in space you're really light,

so astronauts need to buckle up tight.

Rockets go far. Through space they zoom,

reaching as far as the big, round moon.

Down comes the lander with legs out ready

and fiery boosters to hold it steady.

Out come the astronauts to plant their flag

and scoop up samples in their moon-rock bag.

Rockets explore. Through space they roam.

But when they're done, they head back home.

Rockets re-enter in a fiery flash,
to land in the sea with a sizzling splash!

The helicopter carries the brave crew away.
Three cheers for the astronauts:
Hip! Hip! Hooray!

Rocket parts

gravity boots

gravity keeps us on the ground but there is not a lot of gravity on the moon, so astronauts wear these boots to stop them floating away

lunar lander

this takes astronauts down from the rocket to land on the moon

oxygen helmet

we need to breathe oxygen but there isn't any in space, so astronauts carry their own supply which flows into their helmets

fuel tanks

command module

these hold the fuel that makes the rocket go

this is where the astronauts live on their way to and from the moon